PICTURE YOURSELF @ THE TOP

TWEET EYE TRAINING ACADEMY

VOLUME 2 / EDITION 1

BY THE DESIGNERS OF TWEET EYE SOFTWARE

CONTENTS

1

PICTURE YOURSELF @ THE TOP

Welcome to a brave new world where PICTURES are the new currency. **YOU** REALLY can 'PICTURE YOURSELF @ THE TOP'

You can make a living online from simply choosing great pictures and knowing what to do with them.

Very exciting opportunities are happening with Social Media and picture sharing right now.

We live in the age of picture sharing networks, Instagram, Pinterest, Snapchat, Tumblr and many more. Most Social Networks are about sharing photos with friends and family, however these networks have significantly evolved.   These networks are no longer just places where online communities meet, they are now also places where businesses can share product images to promote and build the reputation of their brand.

In **November 2010** a very significant change happened in online commerce, **Facebook exceeded the value of eBay becoming the No.3 U.S web company.**[1] Social media companies are increasingly proving that they can surpass the value of online retail websites and even high ranking search

[1] http://www.bloomberg.com/news/2010-11-15/facebook-passes-ebay-in-value-becoming-no-3-u-s-web-company.html

engines.

In **April 2012** Facebook surprised the world and purchased **INSTAGRAM** the photo filter app just 18 months after its launch for **1 BILLION DOLLARS**.

Instagram isn't the only time Facebook has invested in photo sharing technology. *"Shortly before going public, Facebook closed a deal to hire most employees from Android photo-sharing app developer **Lightbox**. The Lightbox Photos app was promptly shut down and removed from app stores.'* [2]

So what has happened since? **PHOTO SHARING HAS DOUBLED SINCE FACEBOOK'S PURCHASE OF INSTAGRAM IN 2012** WITH *40 MILLION PHOTOS UPLOADED TO INSTAGRAM EVERY SINGLE DAY!*[3]

If you are considering making a career online it is important to understand the two most significant phenomena emerging in social media and how to maximize their usage

1) HARNESS THE POWER OF SHARING IMAGES

2) UNDERSTAND THE NECESSITY TO USE HASHTAGS

One such person who understood this phenomena was an app developer *Ben Silberman who at the age of 27 founded Pinterest in 2010. Pinterest like Instagram is a website where people share photos and hashtag them. Pinterest has become one of the most popular photo sharing websites. Pinterest is now a multi billion dollar company employing over 140*

---

[2] http://www.pocket-lint.com/news/128617-what-does-facebook-own-here-s-the-companies-it-has-acquired-and-the-reasons-why

[3] http://blog.lifecollection.com/photo-sharing-trends/

employees.[4]

Skootle the software developers of the hugely popular TweetAdder software for Twitter recognise that the concepts above can be applied to Instagram too and have launched Followadder a tool that enables people to more easily share **photos** and search **hashtags** on Instagram.

However, you don't have to be a geek or a software company to profit from social media picture sharing. READ ON!

HUGE OPPORTUNTIES ARE POSSIBLE FOR YOU!

Richard Prince - known as the man who steals Instagram photos and resells them for $90,000

Richard Prince is an "artist" whose skill set consists of photographing other people's photographs, adjusting them slightly, and then selling them for enormous profit. He has most recently been known to sell reedited user photos from Instagram for as high as $90,000![5]

- Richard recognized the value of the photos and art that people were sharing everyday for free on photo sharing platforms. He was able to reedit this free resource and sell it on as his own work! Who would have thought that an artist could make an extremely lucrative career from the photos that most people take as snapshots and share for free!

However, you don't have to be connected to rich collectors in the art world to profit from social media

---

4   https://www.fundable.com/learn/startup-stories/pinterest

5   http://bgr.com/2015/05/26/instagram-prints-photos-richard-prince-art/

picture sharing. READ ON!

Tabatha Bundesen - Owner of a Grumpy Cat!

Within days of her cat's first appearance on social media, Tabatha Bundesen, was able to quit her job as a waitress.[6]

- Tabatha had a great picture to share!

The route to success begins from recognizing that you have a great picture to share, or by learning how to profit from great photos and pictures that other people have to share!

If these entrepreneurs can do it so can you!

Most people have the opportunity to gain somewhere in the crazy world of making money from sharing images! Even if you just use the information we are providing you to continue building your brand, attract more viewers or create a more interesting marketing campaign, it will give you a leg up on the competition.

Begin your journey now with the Tweet Eye Training Academy.

To your success!
> Tweet Eye Training Academy

---

[6] http://www.buzzfeed.com/rachelzarrell/grumpy-cats-owner-formerly-a-waitress-says-shes-made-nearly#.kfOZ0A3j9

2

TIPS ON IMAGE USAGE - YOUR LEGAL RESPONSIBILITIES

WORKS PROTECTED BY COPYRIGHT LAW

2.1

If you are considering sharing anything on the internet or social media, you should be aware of the types of work that are protected by copyright law which include

- literary,

- dramatic,

- artistic or musical work,

- the typographical arrangement of a published edition,

- a sound recording,

- a film,

- or a broadcast.[7]

Sharing works that don't belong to you could get

---

 [7] http://en.wikipedia.org/wiki/Copyright_law_of_the_United_Kingdom

you in trouble, unless your sharing of the work abides by the **'Fair Use Exemption' (Section 2.5)**

UNDERSTANDING OWNERSHIP OF IMAGES

THE GENERAL RULE

2.2

Generally speaking, if you take a photograph or create a graphic image you own the copyright on that work and are free to use it on your website, sell duplicates of it, display the work publicly, prepare derivative works based upon that work or even license its use to others.

YOUR LEGAL RESPONSIBILITIES

2.3

There are certain **exceptions to this general rule** however, such as what are known as **"works for hire"**. If you were hired and paid to take photographs or create graphic images, whether as an independent contractor or employee, then you do not own the rights to use such work. A simple example would be a wedding photographer who is paid to take pictures. The photographer does not have the right to use those pictures on his website unless he gets permission from those who hired him to take the pictures.

2.4

Well before the Internet age the **US Copyright Act** governed usage of original works of authorship which, according to Title 17 of the US Code, includes literary, dramatic, musical, pictorial, graphic, motion pictures, audiovisual, sound, architectural, artistic and certain other intellectual works. **The Digital Millennium Copyright Act (DMCA)** attempts to bring more current the existing copyright laws, but does not make major changes in existing law, rather it clarified certain laws and created new laws in reference to the internet and digital age. The DMCA, which was signed into law on October 28, 1998, amended in part the US Copyright Act to provide a limitation on liability for online service providers for copyright infringement, but required such providers to designate an agent to handle claims of copyright infringement.

2.5

FAIR USE EXCEPTION

One exception to use of an image or work that was not created by the person intending to use it is what is known as the **"fair use exception".** Such fair use includes using the work for purposes of criticism, comment, news reporting, teaching, scholarship and research. There are four factors one must consider in determining whether or not a particular use is considered fair use. These factors are

The purpose and character of the use, including whether such use is of a commercial nature or is for nonprofit educational purposes;

The nature of the copyrighted work;

The amount and substantiality of the portion used in relation to the copyrighted work as a whole; and

The effect of the use upon the potential market for, or value of, the copyrighted work. Courts in determining whether or not the fair use exception is valid will consider all the factors in rendering a decision. It is a fact based test and therefore each situation is different and all the factors must be considered as a whole.

ACKNOWLEDGING THE SOURCE IS NO SUBSITUTE FOR OBTAINING PERMISSION

2.6

Acknowledging the source of the copyrighted material does not substitute for obtaining permission

BEST PRACTICE FOR STAYING ON THE CORRECT SIDE OF COPYRIGHT LAW

2.7

The law may seem complex the more you read the regulations, but **probably the best suggestion and advice is that if you do not create the work, then get written permission from the owner to use it for your specific needs**, otherwise visit some of the websites that sell a license to use pictures and graphics.

PICTURES ARE MORE VALUABLE THAN YOU CAN IMAGINE - THE HISTORY OF IMAGE WORTH

Compared to the rise of any other commodity price the value of intellectual property in images and the methods for creating, finding and sharing them has held its own.

3.1

Just how much can a single image be worth?

February 2015, Paul Gauguin 1892 oil painting of two Tahitian girls Nafea Faa Ipoipo (When Will You Marry?) was sold from a Swiss private collection for close to $300 million.

3.2

Just how much can a single photo be worth?

November 2011, another record was set, Rhein II is a photograph made by German visual artist Andreas Gursky in 1999, a print was auctioned for $4.3 million , making it the most expensive photograph ever sold.

3.3

Just how much are picture sharing companies worth?

April 2012, Facebook paid a billion dollars for Instagram

May 2014, Pinterest one of the largest photo sharing networks currently enjoyed for free by over 70 million users, announced that it had secured 200 million in financing boosting its value to 5 billion. Time.com

3.4

FIVE LESSONS A GRUMPY CAT OWNER CAN TEACH YOU!

How did a photo of a Grumpy Cat trigger a multi-million dollar business?

According to some internet articles a waitress was able to give up her day job and began to earn millions when she started sharing photos of her Grumpy Cat.

How did this happen?

LESSON 1 - SHARE YOUR PICTURES!

Fame and fortune began for the Grumpy Cat owner when a photo of their cat was shared on the social news website Reddit in September 2012.

LESSON 2 - MERGE QUOTES WITH YOUR IMAGES!

The photo of the Grumpy Cat became most popular when it was posted with captions.

LESSON 3 - PROTECT YOUR INTELECTUAL PROPERTY!

In January 2013 the owners "Grumpy Cat Limited" applied to the **United States Patent and Trademark** Office to make "Grumpy Cat" a Trademark.

LESSON 4 - PROMOTE & PUBLICIZE!

In May 2013 the Grumpy Cat was recognised as an internet celebrity and was featured on the front page of ***The Wall Street Journal***, and on the cover of ***New York*** magazine in October 2013.

The official Grumpy Cat book *Grumpy Cat: A Grumpy Book* was published on July 23, 2013

The Grumpy Cat 2014 Wall Calendar on July 23, 2013.

By December 2014 the phenomena had grown, "The Official Grumpy Cat" on Facebook had over 7 million "likes".

LESSON 5 - DIVERSIFY YOUR INCOME STREAMS!

The owners wealth increased as requests to make licensed merchandise came into demand

t-shirts, mugs, stuffed toys, "Grumppuccino" iced coffee beverages.

Consider what opportunities exist to make your pictures into merchandise.

Work out what inspires you from the Grumpy Cat owner's story

USING IMAGES TO EARN MONEY ONLINE

The Internet is vast with many opportunities in every field. The **Tweet Eye Training Academy** is focused on showing people how they can use images and pictures to generate revenue online.

5.1

There are many platforms and websites that can be your choice of income – the only requirement is that you must either (a) own your own pictures to make money off of them, i.e. of your own photography, digital art, graphic and logo designing, handmade art, or (b) purchase the right to use pictures from others, etc. Several websites offer different levels of usage for pictures and images.
They include

www.istock**photo**.com,
www.dollarphotoclub.com,
www.shutterstock.com *and*
www.gettyimages.com .

These websites make considerable income form licensing the right to use these images.

Social Sharing

Do not forget that fame and fortune did not begin for the Grumpy Cat owner until they started sharing images of their cat on social media.

5.2

Making an effective strategy for you images to be found on social media is the most important step in beginning to make an online income.

You can directly sell or show off your art work through sites like Facebook, Twitter and Pinterest. Make pages of your art, do a little showingoff about what you can do, and then start selling your pieces to individuals. You can sell your images in different formats like JPEG, TIFF, etc.

The Risks

One of the most valuable lessons to learn from the Grumpy Cat Owner is protect your intellectual property.

5.3

The opportunities that the Tweet Eye Training Academy have identified for you to make money online through using and sharing your images, do come with an element of RISK!

Social Media may be a wonderful way to propel people's interest in what you do, but your intellectual rights to media can potentially become compromised if you do not check the terms and conditions of websites carefully.

"Instagram says it now has the right to sell your photos."

In its first big policy shift since Facebook bought the photo-sharing site, Instagram claims the right to sell users' photos without payment or notification. Oh, and there's no way to opt out."[8]

Do you take photos with a smartphone? Start earning money with them!

More people own mobile phones that easily take digital photos with apps that make it easy to share photos to social networks. There are even apps that will pay you to share your photos.

5.4

For instance there is Clashot and many others emerging like it:

"The free application Clashot gives you an opportunity to create, publish and sell photos taken by a smartphone and earn money if your photo is "liked" by another user.

You'll get income from every sale of each photo, and each shot can be sold an unlimited number of times to an unlimited number of people. As soon as the total of your account exceeds $3, you can withdraw from it in a variety of convenient ways."

---

[8] http://www.cnet.com/uk/news/instagram-says-it-now-has-the-right-to-sell-your-photos/

Ways to Sell Your Images

5.5

Out of many ways, below are listed some of the best ideas that can prove to be profitable as many are using the sources already. If you do not have your own produced images, you can buy some high quality images for cheap rates and then resell them at higher prices. One site to acquire images is Fiverr – many people are willing to sell their pictures at low prices.

Sell your own on **Fiverr**:

Just like you can buy from others, you can also sell your own images on Fiverr to others. These images can be anything: graphic designs, handmade or digital art pieces, pictures of subjects or landscapes, etc.

5.6

5.7

Join affiliate programs Like buying others', affiliate programs are another great way to make money through images even if you do not have your own images to sell. You can simply promote others' images to help them sell and in turn, you get a set amount of commission for every sale they make through you. Affiliate programs are a great way to earn money because you do not need to own or buy images or art to make money – you just need to market them.

Photostock companies Stock photo companies are sites that sell high quality pictures to everyone. On such sites, you can submit your images too, so that every time someone buys it, you get paid.

5.8

Turn your images into items:

If there is one lesson that you can learn from the Grumpy Cat Owner is consider the opportunity to turn your best images into merchandise.

5.9

You do not even need to be approached for a contract or need your own money to get started. There are many sites where you can submit your art to be printed or turned into objects like coffee mugs, frames, t-shirts, pillows, etc. Zazzle and CaféPress are two major sites that allow you to do this.

Whether you are branding a 'Grumpy Cat' or a 'Tweety Bird' think of ways to make your brand more iconic and memorable.

Turn your art into prints: Something every artist would love to see is their art turned into prints. Luckily, there are many opportunities online for this type of art selling. If you upload your images to a **print on demand service** such as

5.10

http://www.lulu.com
http://www.cafepress.com
http://www.society6.com.

Those services will host a shop for you. When people buy the prints the company will print and send them out.

The advantage of these services is that- You don't have to purchase the material & send the prints out. You don't suffer the cost of print mistakes/mess-ups. You don't have to outlay anything for cost of sales such as printers, ink & paper.

The only downside is that you don't make as much profit, it's harder to build your own brand individuality.

Another alternative is to use a company that can help you with marketing and act as your fulfilment center to handle the orders and shipping. You may be able to have the end product produced at less cost and shipped for less than it would cost you to do the work yourself. This would free up your time to concentrate on marketing and sales promotions through Tweet Eye and other marketing campaigns. Compare prices and see what works best for you.[9]

http://lppromoproducts.com/

---

[9] http://leoniedawson.com/how-to-sell-your-artwork-as-prints-online-and-the-hidden-secret-to-success/

5.11

All in all, there are numerous ways for you to sell your talent or work online, or the work which you have purchased the rights off others.

Why not upload your own images or images that you have purchased from sellers on Fiverr to **print on demand service**, and start using Tweet Eye to tweet your print on demand shops today!

COLOURS IN YOUR BRANDING STRATEGY

The Meaning of Colours

The meaning of colours can vary depending on the **culture** in which is being used and **circumstances**.

Brands choose colours very carefully.

Consider the following colours:

Red: is the colour of energy, passion, action, ambition and determination. It is also the colour of anger and sexual passion. Red is an emotionally intense colour which calls for action to be taken.[10] Red is often used in Call To Action phrases and symbols.

---

[10] https://www.linkedin.com/pulse/pyschology-color-marketing-branding-andalusia-media

Blue: is a soothing colour of trust and peace. Brands use it as a way to convey loyalty, integrity, trust, honesty. Considered the safest colour to use by conservative brands.

Yellow: is the colour of the mind and the intellect. It is optimistic and cheerful.

Orange: is the colour of social communication and optimism.

Green: is the colour of balance and growth. It can mean both self-reliance as a positive

Every brand chooses it colours very carefully.

You can get the official colour codes for many famous brands from

http://brandcolors.net/

TOOLS WHICH MAKE THE CREATION OF STUNNING PICTURE CONTENT EASIER

Create your brand identity with typeface, colours, pictures, borders. There are many tools online which will help you create stunning picture content. Many of the resources listed below are free, while others have premium features that you will have to pay for.

7.1

Start creating your brand today with

Free Image Editors 10.2
Free Image Optimizers 10.3
Color Pickers 10.4
Free Typography 10.5

FREE IMAGE EDITORS

Create optimized images for social media turn quotes into visual masterpieces.

7.2

- https://www.canva.com/
- https://pixlr.com/
- http://www.easel.ly/

FREE IMAGE OPTIMIZERS - RESOURCES

Optimize, resize and compress your images online. Tools to help your images load faster.

7.3

- https://tinyjpg.com/
- https://tinypng.com/
- https://compressor.io/
- https://imageoptim.com/

COLOR PICKERS - RESOURCES

- http://flatuicolorpicker.com
- http://coolors.co
- http://couleursapp.com
- http://brandcolors.net
7.4
- http://paletton.com
- http://www.0to255.com
- http://www.colourlovers.com
- http://getuicolors.com
- https://coleure.com
- http://colllor.com

FREE TYPOGRAPHY

Check out these *free commercial fonts and archives.*

7.5

- http://www.typegenius.com
- http://www.fontsquirrel.com
- http://www.fontface.ninja/
- http://www.google.com/fonts
- http://www.dafont.com/
- http://www.1001freefonts.com/
- http://www.fontpark.net/en/#
- http://font-to-width.com/

 ## RECOMMENDED READING

http://thenextweb.com/dd/2015/02/18/300-awesome-free-things-massive-list-free-resources-know/

MAKING MONEY WITH TWEET EYE

For the last two years the **Tweet Eye Training Academy,** have been steadily increasing their income every year simply from sending great photos with hashtags to Twitter.

The **Tweet Eye Training Academy** have used many of the ideas discussed in this book to create businesses using pictures along with smart hashtagging covered in **#Hashtag Your Way To The Top**, to boost the visibility of those businesses on Twitter and increase sales.

Understanding the full potential of using pictures in social media posts containing hashtags will considerably raise the interest you get in your business in future years, as social media becomes more and more the primary way of reaching new business online. Tweet Eye was created with this goal in mind and to provide a simple automated solution.

WHAT IS TWEET EYE?

TWEET EYE is a software application that makes it REALLY EASY to put your website photos into a single tweet or scheduled Tweet campaign. This is the CORE FEATURE of and reason for using Tweet Eye. Currently, some of its

core features are:

AUTOMATION – Tweets with pictures can be set to go out at intervals of between thirty minutes and 24 hours (or even on a random setting). The scheduled tweets can go on for weeks or even months until you cancel or revise them.

TWEET WITH PICTURES EFFORTLESSLY – The software requires you to enter the url you want to promote and brings up the pictures/images from that url. Then you click on the picture or image you want included in your tweet, type in your tweet, choose your hashtags and click "OK".

FREE VERSION – Currently there is a free version available. Silver, Gold and Platinum fee based versions will be released with an estimated launch date of October 1, 2015.

HASHTAG ANALYSIS – For those of you with writer's block the fee based versions will also have a hashtag analysis function to help improve your tweeting.

EASY TO USE – It's so easy even a teenager can use it, just kidding. It's so easy even people over 50 can figure out how to use it . . . seriously!!!

MARKETING – Use Tweet Eye to promote your websites, blogs, social media pages, Etsy and eBay products. (Note: Our testing shows Tweet Eye works with the great majority of websites we have tested.)

We hope you will enjoy the series and other resources of the Tweet Eye brand.

Please feel free to write to us at contact@tweet-eye.com

Also, check out our blog at http://tweet-eye.com/news.htm

The Tweet Eye Training Academy wish you every success!

PICTURE YOURSELF @ THE TOP!

RECOMMENDED READING

#Hashtag Your Way To The Top

www.ingramcontent.com/pod-product-compliance
Lightning Source LLC
Chambersburg PA
CBHW041614180526
45159CB00002BC/857